D1442925

D

Dogs

Collies

by Jody Sullivan Rake
Consulting Editor: Gail Saunders-Smith, PhD

Consultant: Jennifer Zablotny, DVM
Member, American Veterinary Medical Association

Capstone
press
Mankato, Minnesota

Pebble Books are published by Capstone Press,
151 Good Counsel Drive, P.O. Box 669, Mankato, Minnesota 56002.
www.capstonepress.com

1 2 3 4 5 6 12 11 10 09 08 07

Library of Congress Cataloging-in-Publication Data
Rake, Jody Sullivan.
    Collies/ by Jody Sullivan Rake.
    p. cm.—(Pebble Books. Dogs)
    Summary: "Simple text and photographs present an introduction to the collie
breed, its growth from puppy to adult, and pet care information"—Provided
by publisher.
    Includes bibliographical references and index.
    ISBN-13: 978-1-4296-0015-6 (hardcover)
    ISBN-10: 1-4296-0015-2 (hardcover)
    1. Collie—Juvenile literature. I. Title. II. Series.
SF429.C6R35 2008
636.737'4—dc22   2006100686

Note to Parents and Teachers

The Dogs set supports national science standards related to life
science. This book describes and illustrates collies. The images
support early readers in understanding the text. The repetition of
words and phrases helps early readers learn new words. This book
also introduces early readers to subject-specific vocabulary words,
which are defined in the Glossary section. Early readers may need
assistance to read some words and to use the Table of Contents,
Glossary, Read More, Internet Sites, and Index sections of the book.

Table of Contents

Gentle Collies

Collies are gentle dogs
that get along
with other family pets.
They love to work
and play.

Collies are herding dogs.
They help farmers
herd and protect sheep.

From Puppy to Adult

Collies have
six to ten puppies
in a litter.
Collie puppies
grow quickly.

Most puppies chew
on their toys.
But collie puppies
would rather carry
them around.

Collies love lots of attention.
These smart dogs
learn quickly.

Adult collies are about
as tall as a kitchen table.
Collies have long
or short hair.

Taking Care of Collies

Long-haired collies
need to be brushed
every other day.
Short-haired collies should
be brushed once a week.

Collies need to exercise every day. They like to play catch and run outside.

Collies love to spend time with their families.

Glossary

attention—playing, talking, and spending time with someone or something

gentle—kind and calm

herd—to gather animals and keep them together; collies are herding dogs.

litter—a group of animals born at one time to the same mother

protect—to keep safe from danger

Read More

Fitzpatrick, Anne. *Collies.* Dog Breeds. North Mankato, Minn.: Smart Apple Media, 2003.

Kallen, Stuart A. *Collies.* Checkerboard Animal Library. Edina, Minn.: Abdo, 2002.

Internet Sites

FactHound offers a safe, fun way to find Internet sites related to this book. All of the sites on FactHound have been researched by our staff.

Here's how:

1. Visit *www.facthound.com*

2. Choose your grade level.

3. Type in this book ID **1429600152** for age-appropriate sites. You may also browse subjects by clicking on letters, or by clicking on pictures and words.

4. Click on the **Fetch It** button.

FactHound will fetch the best sites for you!

Index

Word Count: 120
Grade: 1
Early-Intervention Level: 16

Editorial Credits
Becky Viaene, editor; Juliette Peters, set designer; Kim Brown, book designer;
    Kara Birr, photo researcher; Karon Dubke, photographer; Kelly Garvin, photo stylist

Photo Credits
Capstone Press/Karon Dubke, 12, 14, 16, 20; Cheryl A. Ertelt, 10; Mark Raycroft, cover,
6; Norvia Behling, 8; Ron Kimball Stock/Ron Kimball, 4; Shutterstock/Rick Dunkerly, 1;
www.jeanmfogle.com, 18

Capstone Press thanks dog trainer Martha Diedrich for her assistance with this book.